MONSTERS!

VAMPIRES

BY PETER CASTELLANO

 Gareth Stevens
PUBLISHING

Please visit our website, www.garethstevens.com. For a free color catalog of all our high-quality books, call toll free 1-800-542-2595 or fax 1-877-542-2596.

Library of Congress Cataloging-in-Publication Data

Castellano, Peter.
 Vampires / Peter Castellano.
    pages cm. — (Monsters!)
 Includes index.
 ISBN 978-1-4824-4095-9 (pbk.)
 ISBN 978-1-4824-4096-6 (6 pack)
 ISBN 978-1-4824-4113-0 (library binding)
 1. Vampires—Juvenile literature. I. Title.
 BF1556.C37 2016
 398'.45—dc23
                              2015031501

First Edition

Published in 2016 by
Gareth Stevens Publishing
111 East 14th Street, Suite 349
New York, NY 10003

Designer: Samantha DeMartin
Editor: Kristen Nelson

Photo credits: Cover, p. 1 Jay P. Morgan/Photodisc/Getty Images; background iulias/ Shutterstock.com; caption box Azuzl/Shutterstock.com; text box Dmitry Natashin/ Shutterstock.com; p. 5 Margaret M. Stewart/Shutterstock.com; p. 7 Dmytro Korolov/ Shutterstock.com; p. 9 serpeblu/Shutterstock.com; p. 11 Lukiyanova Natalia/ Shutterstock.com; p. 13 Unholy Vault Designs/Shutterstock.com; p. 15 (main) Hulton Archive/ Moviepix/Getty Images; p. 17 Hulton Archive/Hulton Archive/Getty Images; p. 19 PHAS/ Universal Images Group/Getty Images; p. 20 Carl savich/Wikimedia Commons; p. 21 Apic/ Hulton Fine Art Collection/Getty Images; p. 23 (inset) ullstein bild/ullstein bild/Getty Images; p. 23 (main) Universal/Moviepix/Getty Images; p. 25 (main) Warner Bros./Moviepix/Getty Images; p. 25 (inset) Mark Cuthbert/UK Press/Getty Images; p. 27 Pictorial Parade/Archive Photos/Getty Images; p. 29 Vera Petruk/Shutterstock.com; p. 30 (vampire) Ekaterina Solovieva/ Vetta/Getty Images; p. 30 (cat) Akimasa Harada/Moment/Getty Images; p. 31 (magic) Ollyy/ Shutterstock.com.

Printed in the United States of America

CPSIA compliance information: Batch #CW16GS: For further information contact Gareth Stevens, New York, New York at 1-800-542-2595.

CONTENTS

A NIGHTMARE

You're asleep in your bed when suddenly you think you hear a noise. Did something move in the corner? You think you see a white face in the moonlight. Does it have **fangs**? It could be a vampire!

BEYOND THE MYTH

A vampire is a **mythical** being that feeds on human blood. Even in a story, it wouldn't be likely to just find one in a bedroom. Most stories say vampires need to be asked to come into a place.

5

VAMPIRE GODDESS

Cultures around the world have believed in vampire myths since as far back as ancient Egypt! The Egyptian goddess Sekhmet was said to drink blood. Egyptians also believed part of a dead person's soul, or *ka*, would feed on the blood of the living sometimes!

BEYOND THE MYTH

Vampire bats are real animals that feed on blood.
Their name likely comes from doing so and the fact
that vampires sometimes turn into bats in stories.

WORLD MONSTERS

What's scarier than a vampire after you at night? A vampire out during the day! In Russian vampire myths, *upirs* (or *upyrs*) can't be harmed by sunlight. Some myths say people who did very bad things in life become *upirs* in death.

BEYOND THE MYTH

The Polish vampire, the *upier*, was said to not only like to drink blood, but also to bathe and sleep in it.

9

The terrifying myth of the *asasabonsam* comes from Ghana. The *asasabonsam* has hooked feet and hangs from trees. When someone walks by, the *asasabonsam* grabs them and uses teeth made of iron to drink their blood—or even eat their whole body!

BEYOND THE MYTH

The Indian myth of Brahmaparusha features a monster drinking blood from people's **skulls** and then eating their brain!

Yara-ma-yha-who also hides in trees to trap those it wants to feed on. It has suckers on its fingers and toes that stick to a person and don't let go. The Yara-ma-yha-who doesn't have fangs. It drinks blood through its suckers!

BEYOND THE MYTH

The myth of Yara-ma-yha-who comes from Australian Aboriginal culture. The Aborigines are the native people of Australia.

MODERN ROOTS

Though vampire myths have been around for centuries, the vampires known best today come from European stories written in the 18th and 19th centuries. At the time, people believed vampires were real, and they were afraid of them!

BEYOND THE MYTH

In ancient Greece, people told stories of beings that bit people as they slept, drinking all the **fluids** from their body.

15

"The Vampyre" by John Polidori was written in 1819. It was about a rich man who drank the blood of young women and then disappeared. Other stories, such as *Varney, the Vampire* and *The Mysterious Stranger*, likely had an effect on the most famous vampire story: *Dracula*.

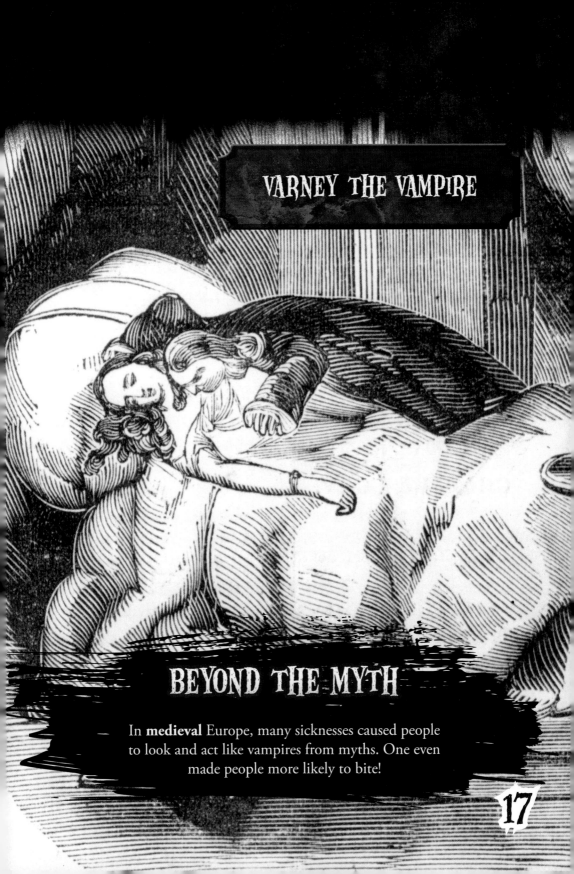

VARNEY THE VAMPIRE

BEYOND THE MYTH

In **medieval** Europe, many sicknesses caused people to look and act like vampires from myths. One even made people more likely to bite!

17

DRACULA

In 1897, Bram Stoker's book about a count from Transylvania brought past and present vampire myths together with great success. In fact, *Dracula* is still what many vampire books and movies base their vampires' features on.

BEYOND THE MYTH

Stoker may have heard stories about 15th-century Transylvanian prince Vlad Dracula and used them in *Dracula*. Dracula was known for leaving his enemies' bodies impaled, or fixed on a sharp stake in the ground.

19

Because Count Dracula was rich and powerful, vampires are often shown as members of the upper class. Dracula also came from eastern Europe, an idea many stories copied. A vampire's ability to control someone's mind or change shape comes from *Dracula*, too.

BEYOND THE MYTH

Elizabeth Bathory was another Transylvanian who may have had an effect on *Dracula*. She was said to bite her maids and bathe in young girls' blood to keep from aging.

21

THE MOVIE

A movie of *Dracula* made Bram Stoker's vampire an even bigger part of popular culture. The 1931 movie starred Bela Lugosi dressed in a suit and cape. That's what most vampire Halloween costumes are based on!

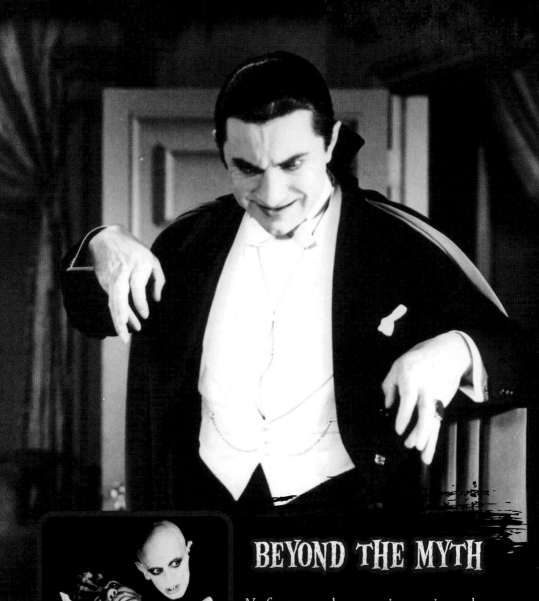

BEYOND THE MYTH

Nosferatu, another vampire movie partly based on Stoker's book, came out in 1922. It's the first time vampires were shown as being harmed by sunlight.

VAMPIRE MANIA!

The movies about vampires don't stop with *Dracula*! In 1994, Brad Pitt starred as a vampire in the movie *Interview with the Vampire*. The cartoon *Hotel Transylvania* and its **sequel** tell the story of a vampire and his monstrous friends.

BEYOND THE MYTH

Between 2008 and 2012, the movies based on Stephanie Meyer's *Twilight* series together made $4.68 billion worldwide.

From *Buffy the Vampire Slayer* to *The Vampire Diaries*, there's a long history of TV shows featuring vampires, too. *Dark Shadows* came before them all in 1966! A vampire named Barnabas Collins is awoken and begins looking for his long lost love.

BEYOND THE MYTH

Dark Shadows was on until 1971. Johnny Depp starred as vampire Barnabas Collins in a 2012 movie based on the show.

KILLING A VAMPIRE

Should you meet a vampire, its good to have a stake handy. It's thought that driving a stake through its heart will kill it. But before you sharpen your stake, you must first believe in this monster. Do you?

BEYOND THE MYTH

Keeping vampires away may be as simple
as wearing garlic or running water! Items of
the Christian faith—such as crosses—are
also said to keep them away.

29

How Do You Become a Vampire?

get bitten by a **VAMPIRE**

catch a certain **ILLNESS**

have a **CAT** jump over your dead body

have a **BIRTHDAY** between Christmas and the Epiphany, January 6

MAGIC

FOR MORE INFORMATION

BOOKS

Baltzer, Rochelle. *Monsters and Other Mythical Creatures.* Minneapolis, MN: Magic Wagon, 2015.

Klepeis, Alicia. V*ampires: The Truth Behind History's Creepiest Bloodsuckers.* Mankato, MN: Capstone Press, 2016.

Tieck, Sarah. *Vampires.* Minneapolis, MN: ABDO Publishing Company, 2016.

WEBSITES

Dracula & Vampire Jokes

kidsjokes.co.uk/jokes/monster/draculajokes.html

Do you love vampires? Learn some jokes about them!

Vampire Bat

kids.nationalgeographic.com/animals/vampire-bat/#vampire-bat-flying-wings.jpg

Read about this real-life vampire that actually feeds on blood.

GLOSSARY

culture: the beliefs and ways of life of a group of people

fang: a long, pointed tooth

fluid: something that flows like a liquid

medieval: having to do with the Middle Ages, a time in European history from about 500 to 1500

mythical: like a legend or story

sequel: a movie or book that comes after another

skull: the boney frame of the head and face

INDEX